·GROWING UP IN·
Ancient Rome

MIKE CORBISHLEY

Illustrated by
CHRIS MOLAN

Troll Associates

Library of Congress Cataloging-in-Publication Data

Corbishley, Mike.
     Growing up in ancient Rome / by Mike Corbishley; illustrated by
Chris Molan.
         p.   cm.
     Includes index.
     Summary: Describes daily life in ancient Rome, discussing family
life, entertainment, schools, religion, and other aspects.
     ISBN 0-8167-2721-X (lib. bdg.)   ISBN 0-8167-2722-8 (pbk.)
     1. Rome—Social life and customs—Juvenile literature. [1. Rome—
Social life and customs.] I. Molan, Chris, ill. II. Title.
DG78.C593   1993
937—dc20   91-14851

Published by Troll Associates

© 1994 Eagle Books

Printed in the U.S.A.

10 9 8 7 6 5 4 3 2 1

Design by James Marks
Edited by Kate Woodhouse

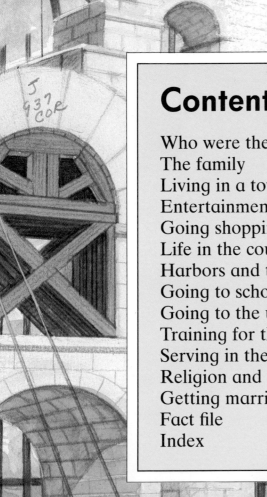

Contents

Who were the Romans?

The Romans came from the center of Italy. They conquered many countries around the Mediterranean Sea until about 60 million people became Romans.

At first, a number of different tribes lived in Italy. Eventually the largest of them, the Latins, became the most powerful. They lived in villages on a group of seven hills overlooking the Tiber River. These villages grew into the city called Rome. The Romans taught their children that Rome was founded by Romulus in 753 B.C.

Later, the Romans drove their kings out and created a *republic*. The people then voted for those they wanted to govern them and lead them into war. But by the first century, the Romans were again governed by a king, who was now called an emperor.

▼ Roman soldiers wore helmets and swords like this in battles across the Empire during the 1st century A.D.

BRITAIN

FRANCE

NÎMES ●
MARSEILLES ●

SPAIN

▲ This map shows the Roman Empire in A.D. 106. It stretched from Britain to Egypt and from Turkey to Spain.

4

► Roman pottery and jewelry has been found all over the Roman Empire.

BLACK SEA

Rome ■

Tiber River

GREECE

TURKEY

CARTHAGE •

MEDITERRANEAN SEA

ALEXANDRIA •

EGYPT

5

The family

The Romans thought the family was very important. Their word for it was *familia*, which included all the relatives in the house and the household slaves. The father was head of the family and the one with power. Women could not vote, but they were important in the running of the house and the buying of food.

The Roman way of life was only possible because they had slaves—people who have had their freedom taken from them. Most household slaves were probably treated well. Others died of hard work on farms or in mines.

▶ Men and boys wore a short-sleeved *tunic* down to the knees. Over that a citizen wore a *toga*. Women wore a long tunic and a dress called a *stola*.

This well-off family lives in a fine house in town, with slaves to wait on them. The house has an inner courtyard to keep it cool in the summer, bedrooms, and more than one dining room. Beyond is an enclosed garden where there is a little shrine to the gods of the household. The children have dolls and miniature models of animals, carts, and people.

Most people in town lived in apartment blocks or above or behind their shops and businesses.

7

Living in a town

Roman towns were busy, bustling places full of houses, apartments, shops, workshops, and public buildings. In new towns or in new parts of old towns, streets were laid out straight. They crossed at right angles to form blocks. The Romans called the blocks *insulae*, which means "islands."

If possible, the streets would be paved with stone and have sewers underground. A proper water supply was available throughout the town. Houses were not usually allowed to have their own water in pipes, but everyone could fetch water from fountains and basins in the streets.

▶ This building is an *aqueduct.* It carried water through a channel at the top from streams in the faraway hills.

The most important area in the town was the *forum*. This was the public square, where business was conducted and markets or meetings were held. Temples to the gods and public buildings were built around it. Richer towns built a wall around the town. Outside the walls, or limits, were cemeteries. Roman law stated that the dead could only be buried outside the town.

Entertainment

Wherever you lived in the Roman Empire, you could enjoy different kinds of entertainment. The Romans' favorite activity probably was going to the public baths. Bathing was not quite what it is today. Men, women, and children spent hours at the baths. They went through a series of rooms, some heated with steam and some with no heat and cold-dip baths. There were pools to splash in and exercise yards. People played dice games there or just chatted. A favorite game for children and adults was played with knucklebones from sheep.

▶ Perhaps the most exciting entertainment was chariot racing in the stadium. It was a dangerous sport, with chariots often crashing.

Theaters were popular and built for large audiences. There were comedies and serious plays, sketches with singing and dancing, and a sort of ballet called a *pantomimus*. The Romans particularly enjoyed the entertainment in the *amphitheater*. They watched trained fighters, called *gladiators*, kill each other for sport. Gladiators also fought wild animals.

11

Going shopping

In Roman towns people went to many different shops. Quite often, the goods for sale were made in a workshop at the back. The bakers, for example, ground flour, made dough, baked it, and sold bread from the counter facing the street.

A Roman woman spent a lot of time buying the groceries and provisions for the family. On shopping trips the girls in the family learned about housekeeping. Advertisements outside the shops showed which had the best offers.

▶ In each street there was a variety of shops. Most of them sold food, but there were also clothes, furniture, and book shops.

12

People tried to buy fresh food, but they also liked spices, herbs, and flavorings to add to meat, fish, and vegetables. One essential ingredient was *liquamen*. This was a strong sauce made from the gills, blood, and insides of fish left with salt to stew in the sun.

The Romans had their main meal, called *cena*, at about four o'clock in the afternoon.

Life in the countryside

The countryside in the Roman Empire provided food for the many people who lived in towns and cities. There were small working farms and large farming estates. Rich Romans grew richer from owning farms, where they built country houses like this one. They left a manager in charge and a housekeeper to look after the house and its slaves.

Some farms grew only one crop. For example, farms in Egypt produced most of the corn needed for bread flour for the people of Rome. If you were traveling through Italy, you might see farms such as this one that grew a mixture of crops like corn, fruit, grapes, and olives. Some farms bred animals, such as cattle, sheep, pigs, and goats, for meat and for their skins.

▼ A *villa* could be a simple farm, a great farming estate, a country house, or a vacation house by the sea. This villa has a house with its own baths, central heating, painted walls, and mosaic floors.

14

The Romans had some simple machinery to help cultivate the land. There was the *vallus*, which was driven by a horse or ox through the corn to cut it. Roman farm slaves used oxen to pull plows and had a variety of cutting and digging tools made of iron.

15

Harbors and trade

The map on pages 4 and 5 shows the extent of the Roman Empire in A.D. 106. There were roads and shipping routes to move goods and produce all over the empire. Goods could be moved fairly quickly—a Roman cargo ship could travel about 100 miles (160 kilometers) in one day. Travel by road was slower. There were carts and carriages for passengers, and caravans of camels crossed the desert. Most produce was taken to local markets, but more important goods were carried over long distances.

▶ This cargo ship is being unloaded at Ostia, the empire's most important port located 15 miles (24 kilometers) from Rome.

Some of the things traded from *Britannia* (Britain) were wool, hides of animals, and hunting dogs. From *Baetica* (southern Spain) came olive oil, fish sauces, and metals. The north African coast traded marble, corn, olive oil, and purple dye for cloth. Wild beasts for the amphitheaters, jewels, ivory, Chinese silks, spices, and perfumes came from the East. Most goods came on cargo ships between 50 and 55 feet (17 and 18 meters) long. A typical load from Spain was about 6,000 large storage jars of olive oil, wine, and fish sauce.

Going to school

In early Roman times, families taught their sons at home. A boy who was to go into public life had to learn outdoor skills and sports as well as how to read and write. He learned to fight in armor, throw the javelin, ride on horseback, swim, and box.

In later times, the wealthy employed an educated slave to teach their children at home. By the age of seven, many boys and girls were also sent to school. A schoolmaster, called a *magister ludi*, set up a class in his house where he taught reading, writing, and arithmetic. Lessons began at dawn, but were finished by the early afternoon.

▼ The Romans wrote with pen and ink on scrolls made of flattened leaves called *papyrus*. Children often wrote on wooden tablets covered with wax with a sharp point called a *stylus*. The other end of the stylus was flat for smoothing the wax surface so it could be used again.

18

Children spent five years at this first school. After that, they were taught by a master called a *grammaticus*. They learned about history, astronomy, geometry, and the literature of Rome and Greece. Pupils were taught to speak clearly and had to recite texts such as *Aesop's Fables* in front of the class. Some schools offered gymnastics as part of the curriculum.

Going to the university

Some young people, almost always boys, went on to a final stage of education at the age of 16. We would call this the university. Roman universities were centers where students studied with several different scholars.

The family chose one of several towns for their sons' higher education. The Greeks had already established a number of centers of education long before the Roman period. The Romans admired the literature and art of the Greeks.

▶ Teachers of rhetoric conducted their lectures and discussions in the open. They liked the courtyards of a *gymnasium,* which was a training area for athletes, and the forum.

Cicero, a famous Roman lawyer and politician, tells how he went to Athens to study. For further learning, he went to Asia Minor (now called Turkey), and then to the Greek island of Rhodes.

Young men needed to learn the art of *rhetoric* if they were to enter public service in the law or in government. Rhetoric was the art of public speaking. Teachers trained their students to speak well and clearly, and to present a difficult question and to argue their case.

Training for the army

The Romans needed a large army to control their huge empire. A young man joined a *legion* of about 5,500 men and was put into a *century* (100 men). He was taught to march long distances with heavy loads. A Roman soldier carried a pack weighing about 66 pounds (30 kilograms). In it were his rations and tools for making the camp. On a march in wartime, a camp was made every night. Soldiers used pickaxes and shovels to dig out a ditch and construct a great bank of earth around the tents.

▶ A soldier learned how to swim and ride fully armed. He was trained in javelin throwing and stone slinging. The new recruit practiced hand-to-hand fighting with a wooden sword and shield.

Soldiers served in the legion for 25 years. They were paid, but they had to provide their own food, weapons, and armor. Each year two officials called *consuls* were voted in charge of the army. Each legion had a commander, called a *legatus,* who had six officers called *tribunes* serving him. The soldiers were trained by *centurions*.

23

Serving in the provinces

Under the emperors the Roman Empire got bigger and bigger. At its biggest, there were nearly 450,000 soldiers defending the frontiers and providing a police force for the people.

But it was not only soldiers who were needed to control the empire. A young man could expect to serve both in the army and as a junior official in the provinces. He would gradually gain experience in different posts and might reach the highest office—one of the two consuls who were the chief officials, chief magistrates, and army commanders.

▶ The governor often consulted the emperor in Rome. One governor, for example, asked whether a town should be allowed a fire service. If people disagreed with their governor, they could write to the emperor.

Each province in the empire was governed by a legatus, who was the governor and commander-in-chief of the army in the province. The legatus had a staff of between 30 and 40 officials. There were secretaries and messengers, lawyers, clerks, personal assistants, and army officers. A *procurator* looked after all the financial affairs of the province. Everyone had to pay taxes to Rome. The legatus and his staff had to travel through the province to see that everything was in order and report back to the emperor.

Religion and ceremonies

The Romans believed in many gods, goddesses, and spirits. They believed the gods controlled everything, so it was important to make them offerings and sacrifices. They built magnificent temples and had altars in their homes.

When a boy "came of age," he dedicated his *bulla* (a lucky charm he had worn around his neck since birth) and his boy's toga to the gods. On the eve of her marriage, a girl dedicated her toys to the gods of the household.

▶ The *Saturnalia* was held on December 17. People are waiting for the emperor to sacrifice an ox, a sheep, and a pig.

As the Romans believed in a number of gods, they did not mind people worshipping "new" gods. One popular god, especially among soldiers and merchants, was Mithras. The worship of Mithras came from Persia in the first century A.D.

A new religion, Christianity, began in the first century. At first the Roman emperors objected to it as it seemed to threaten Roman rule, so they persecuted Christians. But Christianity became the official Roman religion in A.D. 312.

Getting married

The life of Roman women was centered around the home. The richer women had female slaves to look after them and to help run the house. Both boys and girls married at a younger age than most people do today. The girl was usually about 12 and the boy 14. Marriages were usually arranged by the parents and followed by a special engagement ceremony, called the *sponsalia*. Choosing the right wedding day was important. The second half of June was thought to be the luckiest time.

There were different marriage ceremonies, but the most popular kind was held at the girl's home.
The bride said to her husband, *"Ubi tu Gaius, ego Gaia,"* which means, "Whichever family you belong to, I also belong." The guests all shouted *"Feliciter!"* – "Good luck!"

The husband then led his wife to their new home and carried her over the threshold for good luck. The wife joined the other women of the family, and together they cared for the young children.

It is not our custom to marry at such a young age. But many other aspects of Roman life—from their sturdy roads to their fascinating language—are still important parts of our world today.

◄ The birth of a child had to be registered within 30 days. A girl was named on the eighth day after birth, a boy on the ninth. Romans had three names. The first was a given name, for example, Flavia or Cornelia for girls and Marcus or Sextus for boys. The second name showed the person's tribe, and the third was the family name.

Fact file

Roman writing

We can still read actual Roman writing today, 2,000 years after the Roman period. Some books and letters have survived, mostly because the papyrus has been preserved in the hot, dry climate of Egypt. Roman inscriptions cut into tombstones or other monuments can be seen in museums today. Other Roman writings have been preserved because monks in the medieval period copied Roman and Greek manuscripts that have now rotted away.

The Latin language

Many of the words we use today in English come from the Latin spoken by the Romans. Here are some you will know: doctor, actor, horror, circus, animal, area. Look through this book and find other Latin words that have changed slightly. For example, *Britannia* (Britain), *familia* (family).

◄ The bronze dog tag says "Hold me if I run away, and return me to my master Viventius on the estate of Callistus."

► Amphitheaters were built to hold very large audiences. The largest in the Roman empire was called the Colosseum. It could hold 50,000 people. Smaller amphitheaters in the provinces held as many as 20,000 people.

Looking for the Romans

You will find lots of evidence from the Roman period today in Europe and the Mediterranean area, in what was once the Roman Empire. Museums often have collections of everyday Roman objects, statues, and tombstones. You can also find Roman buildings. To this day, Roman roads are still used as main routes in Great Britain.

Roman temples were often converted into churches. For example, the Pantheon in Rome was built as a temple to all the gods. It has been used as a Christian church since A.D. 609.

Roman amphitheaters are still used for entertainment today. The amphitheater at Nîmes in the south of France is now used for bullfights.

Index

32